Contents

Words appearing in the text in bold, **like this**, are explained in the Glossary.

The Victorian age

The Victorian age is named after Queen Victoria, who became Britain's queen in 1837 and reigned until her death in 1901. During this time, Britain became the richest and most powerful nation in the world. The **British Empire** included a quarter of the world's land and people. British ideas and inventions were taken to many other countries, while the British Empire provided wealth and jobs for people in Britain.

A land of towns and cities

During Victoria's life, Britain went through startling changes. Britain's population of 15 million in 1801 increased to more than 37 million by 1901. During the **Industrial Revolution**, many people moved from the country to work in new factory towns and cities. In 1801 about 30 per cent of British people lived in towns. By 1901, about 80 per cent did so. London was Europe's biggest city, with over 7 million people.

Victorians were proud of the British Empire, which was ruled by Queen Victoria. The countries of the empire are shown in red on this map from the time.

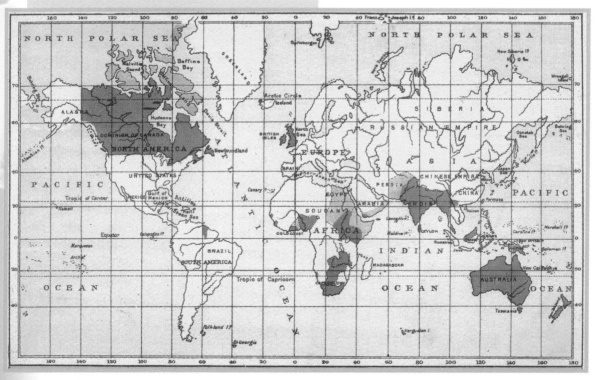

Goods made in Britain's factories were carried overseas in ships built in British shipyards. The port of London, shown here, was crowded with sailing ships and new iron steamships, bringing food and raw materials (such as timber, iron, cotton) to Britain.

Rich and poor

Most people in Victorian Britain had to work or go hungry. The poorest people lived in wretched city **slums** or tiny cottages. People who worked on farms and in factories belonged to the **working class**. Many had to fight hard to win better conditions and higher wages from their employers.

Many **middle-class** people, such as doctors and shopkeepers, lived comfortably in houses in the **suburbs** of towns. The rich **upper classes** included the aristocracy (landowners such as dukes) and new factory owners.

Pioneers in a new age

In this book, you will discover the kind of jobs Victorians did. Many jobs were still done by hand, but other workers had to learn to use new machinery. Some jobs were completely new, such as driving a steam train or **typing** letters. The Victorians thought that work was good for people and for society. Many believed that work was the key to progress, making life better for everyone.

Victorian money

Wages were paid in pounds (£), shillings (s) and pence (d). A typical working man in the 1840s might earn about 15 shillings (75p in today's money) a week. He would spend about 3 shillings and sixpence (17p) each week on bread and about 2 shillings and sixpence (12p) on rent.

Jobs and the jobless

When the Victorian age began, most of Britain's 15 million people worked on farms. By 1850, things were very different. Many people had moved to the towns, to work at machines in new factories. The **Industrial Revolution** had made Britain the 'workshop of the world'.

Working in factories

By the 1850s, more than one million men, women and children worked in cotton or woollen mills in northern England. Parents and children often had jobs in the same mill. They learned new skills to work the machinery. Factory owners liked to employ women and children for delicate work, but paid them less than men. Factories were often dangerous and unhealthy places. There were no laws to protect workers, until the new Factory **Acts** improved matters (see page 21).

This picture shows men in Marylebone workhouse in London. Old people dreaded ending their days in a workhouse. There was hard work to do and you went hungry if you broke the rules.

The workhouse

Unlike today, people without jobs received no money from the government. The jobless poor either roamed the country as **beggars** or were sent to the **workhouse**. Life in a workhouse was made unpleasant to keep out scroungers (the 'lazy and work-shy'). People were put to work breaking up stones or untwisting lengths of old rope. Their food was mostly bread and potatoes. Most poor people hated the very name 'workhouse'.

Law and order

Many factory towns were rough and lawless. Before 1829, Britain had no proper police. People without jobs sometimes took to crime, risking harsh punishments. A man could be hanged for sheep stealing. For catching a rabbit to feed his family, a hungry farm worker could be arrested for **poaching** and sent to Australia for seven years.

Workers could not vote in elections for Parliament. To demand fair laws, they had to take to the streets and protest. When soldiers were called out to keep order, peaceful protests sometimes turned into riots. After local police forces were set up, however, factory towns became more peaceful.

Peelers take to the streets

Sir Robert Peel (1788–1850) set up London's police force in 1829. At first, Londoners made fun of the 'peelers' or 'bobbies', who were paid 3 shillings (15p) a day, but the streets soon became safer. On 5 November 1829, Sir Robert Peel wrote to the Duke of Wellington (the prime minister): 'I want to teach the people that freedom does not consist in having your house robbed by organized gangs of thieves and in leaving the main streets of London in the nightly possession of drunken women and layabouts.'

London policemen were nicknamed 'bobbies' or 'peelers' after Sir Robert Peel. They wore blue coats and trousers and, until 1864, top hats. The first policemen blew whistles to raise the alarm.

City clerks

Running the **British Empire** created new jobs in the offices of the **civil service**. Increased **trade** between Britain and the countries of the Empire also led to more jobs in banks and offices. Victorian London became a centre of world business. People doing office work were called clerks and, until quite late in the 19th century, most clerks were men. Office work was very different from what we know today.

The Victorian office

There were no telephones on Victorian office desks until the late 1880s. Errand boys ran with urgent messages. Sending messages speeded up in the 1840s with the invention of the **telegraph**, and the new 'penny post' (letters with stamps on). There were no computers or photocopiers – in fact, not even any electricity in offices until the 1880s. Clerks wrote letters and copied out figures by hand. Some used old-fashioned **quill pens**, but wooden pens with metal nibs and (from the 1880s) fountain pens, containing their own supply of ink, became more common. In the 1870s, typewriters began to be used.

A clerk's work often involved copying out letters and business documents. Though paid less than £100 a year, clerks were expected to look tidy. They wore white collars, which is why we use the expression 'white-collar worker' to refer to an office worker today.

London's rush hour begins

London woke up every morning to the creak of cartwheels and the crunch of boots on cobbled pavements as thousands of office workers went to their jobs. For the first time, large numbers of people became **commuters**, working in the city but living out in the **suburbs**. It was the beginning of the rush hour.

In the 1830s, the first steam-driven coaches began carrying passengers into central London from outlying districts. In 1829, George Shillibeer started his horse-pulled 'Omnibus' service. Each bus carried 20 people – *omnibus* is a Latin word meaning 'for all'.

London clerks could also take a steam train to work. The Metropolitan Railway, opened in 1863, was the first 'underground' line. Trams came along in the 1870s, but it was not until 1899 that Londoners could go to work on petrol-engined buses.

Rush-hour traffic on London Bridge in around 1890. Horse-drawn carts hauled heavy goods, while people rode in horse buses, cabs and carriages. Cart horses ate from nosebags as they worked, and drank water from troughs at the roadside.

Farm workers

Victorian farmers grew more food than ever before in Britain's history, but new machines meant fewer jobs for farm labourers. In 1871, there were one million farm workers, paid low wages. Many farm workers left the countryside, looking for better-paid jobs in towns. By 1901, there were only 600,000 farm workers in Britain.

Muscles and machines

Many farm workers still used hand-tools, like long-bladed scythes, for cutting crops. However, farmers were urged to try farm improvements, such as chemical fertilizers and steam engines. Some farmers introduced steam-pulled ploughs and mechanical reapers for cutting wheat.

Most farms had horses to pull ploughs and carts, or haul tree trunks. In some districts, such as Sussex, ploughmen drove teams of **oxen**.

Men and women worked together in the farmers' fields at harvest time. Men wore hats and women harvest workers wore bonnets to protect their heads from the sun.

Dirty from dawn till dusk

Threshing was a dusty job that most farm workers hated. The writer W H Hudson heard of a thresher known as Old Reed, who worked near Salisbury in the 1830s: 'from earliest dawn till after dark he would sit or stand in a dim, dusty barn, monotonously pounding away, without rest and without dinner, and with no food but a piece of bread and a pinch of salt'. Old Reed was paid 8 shillings (40p) a week. He saved hard and left his daughters £100 when he died!

Farming skills

Farm workers sought new jobs at 'hiring fairs' in country towns. To show what they did, shepherds carried their crooks (curved sticks for hooking sheep), while carters (cart-drivers) wore a strip of whipcord in their hats. Farmers picked out whichever workers they needed.

Shepherds roamed the hills with their sheepdogs, often sleeping in huts on wheels in the fields during spring lambing. Caleb Bawcombe, a Wiltshire shepherd, took charge of his father's flock at the age of six. Many other boys did the same. Cowmen got up at 4 a.m. for morning milking. Fresh milk was left in large cans called churns at the farm gates, to be collected by town dairies, while dairymaids used some of it to make cheese and butter at the farm. Cattle, sheep, pigs and geese were driven to market by drovers. A drover's walk from Norfolk to London took a week but, by the 1850s, many animals were sent to market by train.

Seasonal pickings and mowing teams

Seasonal farm work provided jobs for men, women and children. In spring, they cleared fields of stones, ready for planting. In summer and autumn, they picked ripe crops such as apples and cut cereal crops by hand, working in teams. They were often in the fields from 6 a.m. until 8 p.m. or later.

Country craftworkers

Country people used many skills in their work. Some crafts had changed little since the Middle Ages – shoeing a horse, for example, or making the wooden wheels for a farm wagon. The skills of the blacksmith and wheelwright were handed down from father to son, and from master-craftsman to **apprentice**. By the end of the 19th century, however, the countryside had changed. Tractors began to replace horses, and lorries took over from wagons. Old crafts were disappearing.

The blacksmith

The village blacksmith made and repaired iron tools, such as spades and ploughs. He also made and fitted iron horseshoes to horses' hooves – a job blacksmiths still do today. His workplace was the smithy. Inside was a fire of coal or charcoal, known as the forge. The blacksmith puffed air into the fire with bellows (a baglike air pump), until it was red-hot. Then he heated metal in the fire to soften it. He hammered the soft metal into shape, before plunging it into water to cool it. With its noise, flames and steam, the smithy must have seemed a magical place to children.

A blacksmith making a horseshoe. The forge was kept red-hot by bellows which blew air into the fire. The smithy rang to the sound of the smith's hammer as he worked.

A farm wagon could carry up to 4 tonnes. Its wheels were often almost 2 metres across. Driving a wagon pulled by a team of powerful horses took skill and strength.

The wainright and wheelwright

Wagons were made by local wainwrights. ('Wain' is an old name for wagon.) These carts had to be strong, because they carried all heavy loads. The wheelwright made wheels for the wagon. He used elm-wood (which would not split) for the centrepiece, into which he fitted spokes of tough oak. Ash was best for the curved sections of the outer wheel, because ash wood would 'give' as the wheel bounced along bumpy lanes. To finish the wheel, an iron tyre was fitted around it.

Lost crafts

Many Victorian country crafts have died out. The pump-maker drilled out the inside of an elm branch, to make a water pump for a cottage. The cordwainer made shoes, belts, harnesses and other leather goods. Coopers made wooden barrels for beer and cider. Travelling workers called tinkers mended metal buckets and watering cans.

Dusty work

Wood was needed to make houses, furniture, fencing and wagons. Men who cut tree trunks into planks for timber were called sawyers and they worked over a pit. One man (the boss) stood on top, holding one end of a long metal saw. The junior sawyer had to stand in the pit, holding the other end of the saw. As he pulled at his end, sawdust fell on his head.

Health workers

It was easy to fall ill in Victorian Britain, but less easy to get well again. Poor people often could not afford a doctor's bills. Hospitals were badly run and dirty. Surgeons had no **anaesthetics** and often did not wash their hands or instruments between operations. Nurses had no proper training. The streets were filthy, and so was the drinking water. However, things started to improve from the 1850s. There were new anaesthetics and antiseptics (to prevent infection), better medical training for doctors and nurses and cleaner hospitals and towns.

A doctor attends a sick child. Before the telephone was widely used in the 20th century, people called the doctor by sending a note with a runner or with a rider on horseback.

Men and women in medicine

Although women could act as **midwives**, they could not train as nurses until 1860, when Florence Nightingale (1820–1910) founded Britain's first training school for nurses. Elizabeth Garrett Anderson overcame many obstacles to qualify as Britain's first woman doctor in 1870.

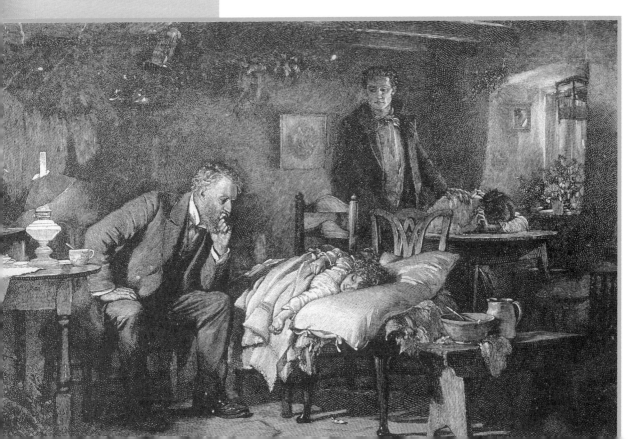

Most poor people did without a doctor. When sick, they went to an apothecary (a chemist) or bought pills and medicines from shops. Traditional healers, often women, could suggest cures (such as plant medicines) for practically every ill. These treatments were not always a success.

Cleaning up the mess

Main streets in cities were kept clean by roadsweepers and rubbish collectors. 'Nightsoil men' carted away waste from **cesspits**, but backstreets and alleys were often stinking. Drains were clogged and water pipes awash with germs.

In 1832, a terrible disease called **cholera** struck Britain, killing more than 20,000 people. Cholera returned in 1848 and 1853. John Snow, a London doctor, found that 50 people were dying every day in one district of London. They were all drinking water from the same water pump. He removed the pump handle so that nobody could drink the cholera-carrying water – and nobody else in that district fell sick with the dreaded disease.

Britain's first Public Health Act (1848) was passed to clean up town drains and water. In 1871, a surgeon named Sir John Simon was put in charge of public health. After 1875, every town had a doctor as its medical officer, and a public health inspector (called an Inspector of Nuisances). They made sure that children were **vaccinated**, that drinking water was clean and that rubbish was cleared away from the streets and alleys.

Wonderful pain relievers

In 1846, a surgeon named Robert Liston gave a patient a drug called ether, to make him unconscious, before cutting off his leg. The patient woke up when it was all over, asking when the surgeon would start. He had just had the first operation in Britain under a general anaesthetic. Queen Victoria was given a safer anaesthetic, chloroform, in 1853, while giving birth to her eighth baby. She found the pain relief 'wonderful'.

Engineers and apprentices

The Victorians were great **engineers.** They mixed traditional skills with new ways of working, using horses alongside steam engines. They also worked fast. Joseph Paxton, who had been a gardener, designed the Crystal Palace for the **Great Exhibition** of 1851 (see the picture on page 42). No one had ever used so much iron and glass in a building, yet he planned the huge structure in just ten days.

New landscapes

Thomas Telford and James Brindley built roads and canals that altered Britain's landscape. Telford had been a stonemason's **apprentice** before becoming an engineer. Robert Napier, a Scottish engineer, built engines for big new ocean liners. His work helped to make Scotland's River Clyde famous for shipbuilding, creating jobs for many men around the city of Glasgow over the next 100 years.

The most famous of all Victorian engineers was Isambard Kingdom Brunel (1806–1859). Brunel designed and built the Clifton Suspension Bridge near Bristol, much of the Great Western Railway and what was then the world's biggest ship, the *Great Eastern*.

Isambard Kingdom Brunel's gigantic steamship *Great Eastern* (shown here under construction) was so big that, in 1858, it had to be launched sideways into London's River Thames.

The Forth Railway Bridge across the Firth of Forth in Scotland took seven years to finish (1883–90). Its builders put together 50,000 tonnes of metal to form the great spans of the bridge, resting on natural rock and concrete islands sunk in the waters of the Forth.

Such engineers led teams of workers busily digging, tunnelling, **rivetting** and bricklaying. Gangs of men with shovels, horses and steam engines built the Thames Embankment and Blackwall Tunnel in London, the Forth Bridge in Scotland, and other marvels of their age. In towns, they laid new drains and water mains, pipes for gas-lighting in homes and, later, electricity cables.

Learning the trade

Boys learned the skills of their trade, from shipbuilding to shoemaking, by becoming apprentices. Training 'on the job' from a skilled worker could take five years. During this time a boy would be given food and a place to stay in return for working for his 'master'. Good employers saw that apprentices were trained properly, but some took on homeless boys simply as cheap labour.

The apprentice boy

The local **workhouse** paid for the food and clothing of one poor apprentice. Records for 1873 from a Welsh workhouse tell us that 'Evan Jones, a pauper child… be bound an apprentice to Peter Jones of Llanerfil to learn the trade of a shoemaker for three years'. The 1871 **census** shows that Evan Jones was no older than eleven. A note says that a workhouse official had to 'see that the apprentice is supplied with the clothing so allowed'.

Railway builders

The railway age began in 1830, when steam **locomotives** of the Liverpool and Manchester Railway pulled passengers in carriages for the first time. By 1838, trains were running from London to Birmingham. Soon there were railway lines all over Britain, and in many other countries.

The railway builders

The most famous Victorian railway **engineer** was George Stephenson (1781–1848), who never went to school and was eighteen before he could pay for lessons in reading and writing. By then he was an engineer in a coal mine, where crude steam engines were used to haul coal wagons. Stephenson built his first steam locomotive in 1814. In 1829, he and his son Robert built the *Rocket*, which won a speed-trial against three other engines when it reached a record speed of 48 kph. Stephenson engines pulled the new trains on the Liverpool and Manchester Railway.

A navvy army

Railways were laid by gangs of workers with picks, shovels and hammers. They also dug tunnels, built bridges and put up **viaducts**. In 1847, there were more than 200,000 of these navigators (or 'navvies' – a name first used in the 1700s for the diggers of Britain's canals). Armies of railway navvies moved around the country, living in camps and shacks. They were famous for getting drunk and frightening villagers, much as the new steam engines used to frighten the horses.

Here railway workers are clearing ground to put down wooden sleepers. Cuttings and tunnels were dug to take the tracks through hills.

Working on the railway

The railways created many new jobs. Practical, sober men were preferred for engine drivers. Isambard Kingdom Brunel said in 1841, 'It is impossible that a man that indulges in reading should make a good engine-driver.' Firemen shovelled coal to turn water into pressurized steam in the engine's boiler. Guards rode in the brake vans. Signalmen waved flags by day and coloured oil-lamps at night to tell trains to stop or go – until moving-arm signals were introduced in the 1840s. By then, many towns had their own railway station, complete with **porters**, ticket clerks and a **stationmaster**.

This painting by W P Frith (1862) shows a busy platform at London's Paddington Station. By this time, millions of passengers were travelling by train and thousands of people had jobs on the railways.

Railway mania

Early in Queen Victoria's reign, people went railway mad. In one year alone, 1845, Parliament was asked to pass 1200 plans for new railways. Fortunes were made, and lost. Words such as 'train', 'station', 'ticket collector' and 'signalman' were in common use by 1850. So was 'overtime', as navvies were paid extra money for extra hours worked.

Factory workers

✢ ✢

In 1770, James Hargreaves' new 'spinning jenny' machine allowed a single worker to spin sixteen cotton threads at the same time. By the 1830s, a steam spinning-machine with one worker could spin over 2000 threads at once. Such was the pace of the **Industrial Revolution**.

Toiling in the factory

With the factory age came a new kind of job. Instead of working at home, most people were paid weekly wages to go to work in a factory. Factory workers made every object imaginable: steam engines, printing presses, machine tools, weaving **looms**, bicycles, typewriters, rifles, teapots, toilets, and millions of screws, nuts and bolts and nails.

Skilled workers, such as hand-weavers, were no longer wanted. Unskilled women and children were. Workers had to keep up with the speed of the machines, or they would lose their jobs. The only day off was Sunday. Each year there was a week's holiday, when the factory shut down for the machines to be repaired.

Workers in factories, mills and ironworks toiled for long hours with little time off. Paintings of industry might show 'labour' as noble and useful, but jobs were often boring and dangerous.

Many workers lived in rented rooms or cheap houses built by the factory owner. Robert Owen built a 'model factory' at New Lanark in Scotland, providing his workers with decent homes, vegetable gardens and schools. In 1853, Sir Titus Salt built a new mill and workers' homes at Saltaire, away from smoky Bradford. Such **reformers** showed that it was possible to treat workers well and still make money.

Dangerous work

Most factories were noisy, dusty and dangerous. Steam hissed, pistons pounded, looms clattered, wheels spun and looping belts whirled. Many workers were hurt by hot, fast-moving machinery. Others were made ill by soot, smoke, metal dust or chemicals. Small children scrambled under machines while they were still working to fix broken threads or oil moving parts.

Life-saving Acts

Lord Shaftesbury (1801-85) persuaded Parliament to pass the first Factory **Act** in 1833. This fixed an hourly limit for child-workers, and forced owners to let inspectors check working conditions in their factories. At first there were just four inspectors for the whole country. More Factory Acts followed, making factory jobs safer.

At a typical factory, the bell would ring at 6 or 7 a.m., calling workers from the rows of little houses close by. The first work **shift** lasted six hours. Then there was a short meal break before a second six-hour shift. In the evening, the workers cleaned their machines before walking home, very tired.

Sir Titus Salt's mill at Saltaire in Yorkshire. Workers' homes built by Salt were close enough for them to get to the mill easily.

Sweatshops

Even in the factory age, some people still worked at home. Partly made clothes from a factory were finished by home workers. This was known as 'sweated labour'. The dingy rooms in their houses in which they worked were called sweatshops.

Stitched up

In 1848, the journalist Henry Mayhew uncovered a scandal in the clothing trade. Shops were selling cheaper, factory-made clothes at the price of suits and dresses made by a skilled **tailor** or **seamstress.** Factory owners handed unfinished clothes to a 'sweater', who shared out the finishing work between handworkers. One sewed on buttons, another cuffs, a third pockets and so on. Most workers were women at home, often struggling to raise families alone. The sweater paid them as little as possible.

Some families did work at home to add a few pennies to their small weekly income. Children were expected to help before and after school (if they went to school). This mother is getting some help making small brushes.

Women were paid just 5 shillings (25p) a week for cutting and stitching. They had to pay out 3 shillings (15p) for trimmings (cloth), candles and coal for the fire (they needed hot irons to press the clothes). This left 2 shillings (10p) a week to live on. A verse by Thomas Hood called *The Song of the Shirt*, first published in the magazine *Punch* in 1843, summed up their plight:

'With fingers weary and worn,
With eyelids heavy and red
A woman sat, in unwomanly rags
Plying her needle and thread'

Sweating in other trades

Sweated workers made straw hats in Luton, cut leather for shoes in Northampton and finished wooden penholders in Birmingham. In the 1890s, one Birmingham woman reported that she earned less than 2 pennies (1p) for making 144 penholders. She worked in her kitchen, helped by her children. Each penholder was rubbed smooth with sandpaper and then given five coats of varnish with a sponge.

By 1900, campaigns by **trade unions** and laws fixing minimum wages for home workers ended the worst of sweated labour in Britain. It continued in some **trades**, however. It is still a problem today in many poor countries, for example, in the clothing and shoe industries.

Coal miners

❖ ❖

By 1848, Britain's factories and railways were burning 50 million tonnes of coal a year – three times as much as in 1815. By 1890, it was 180 million tonnes. Coal was burned to heat homes. It was also used to make **coke** for iron making, and coal gas for lighting and heating. In the 1880s, there were about 500,000 coal miners in Britain.

Down the mine

Victorian miners cut coal by hand, in mines dug deep to reach layers of coal hundreds of metres underground. Miners travelled down a long vertical shaft in lifts called cages. In some coal mines, they went down clinging to a chain, their feet resting in wire loops.

Miners often worked bent double, or on their stomachs in cramped tunnels, hacking at the coal with picks. Other workers hauled lumps of coal away in carts or in baskets. Until 1842, women and children also worked underground, dragging small coal wagons.

Coal miners worked with pick and shovel, often deep underground. The safety lamp shown, invented in 1815, stopped a naked flame causing a gas explosion.

This newspaper report tells of a mining accident in South Wales on 23 June 1894. There were many such tragedies, but with no other jobs for them, survivors usually had to go back down the pit.

The dangers of minework

Miners worked in terrible conditions, choking on coal dust and soaked through by water dripping into the tunnels. Many were killed or hurt in a tunnel collapse, a flood or fire. Unseen 'pockets' of poisonous gas could choke miners, so men took caged canary birds into the mine tunnels. If the bird 'passed out', they knew poisonous gas was very near.

Mining communities

Miners lived close to the mine, in villages where almost every man – and his sons – went 'down the pit'. A 'knocker-up' walked from house to house to wake the men on the early **shift**, often before dawn. When the men came home, they were black with coal dust.

A strong 'hewer' or coal-cutter was 'king', so long as he escaped injury or illness. But by the time he was in his forties, a miner was too old to cut coal. He ended his days doing surface work, helping the women known as 'pit brow lassies' to pick out stones from the coal.

In addition to 286 men, 120 horses were killed in this disaster.

TERRIBLE COLLIERY DISASTER AND GREAT LOSS OF LIFE

One of the most appalling disasters ever known in the South Wales coalfield occurred on Saturday afternoon at the Albion Colliery, Cilfynydd, near Pontypridd, in the Taff Valley. The colliery belongs to a limited liability company, and employs altogether about 2,000 men and boys. During the great coal strike, when troops were imported into South Wales to quell the riots, it was selected as the headquarters of the cavalry. Although practically a new one, the colliery is one of the largest in South Wales, and it has been exceptionally free from accidents hitherto. The pit is ventilated by a steel fan, and the depth of the shaft is 520 yards. It appears that on Saturday the afternoon shift had gone down to work at about 2 o'clock, while a number of the day shift worked on. It is known that 13 cages descended the shaft, each containing at least 20 men, and it is computed that altogether between 260 and 280 men were in the pit at the time of the disaster. It was fortunate enough that it was Saturday afternoon, when the shift would necessarily be a comparatively small one, for of the 260 men said to have descended at 2 o'clock only 16 are known to be alive. About a quarter to 4 o'clock a loud report was heard, followed almost immediately by another, and the mouth of the pit was immediately enveloped in thick black smoke, through which tongues of flame shot into the air. The concussion on the surface was tremendous, and the force of the blast was so great that the top of the pit was completely blown to pieces, and large balks of timber were hurled about in every direction. One of the huge beams fixed across the shaft, measuring 20ft. by 15in. square, was blown upwards, but fortunately the stoppage of the fan was only momentary. The down-cast shaft was damaged as well as the up-cast. In a short time the colliery yard was filled by thousands of people in a state of intense excitement. The necessary preparations were hastily made for descending the pit, and scores of volunteers willingly came forward to take part in the work of rescue. The manager of the colliery (Mr. P. Jones) in company with the pitman and a few others went down the shaft first. They found the bottom very much damaged, and several empty trams were lying about. They also saw a couple of dead horses. Later explorers discovered eight men alive and 13 dead within a hundred yards of the bottom of the shaft. Meanwhile medical aid had been summoned, and Dr. Lytle, Dr. Leckie, and others were soon on the spot and descended the shaft. The wounded having been attended to at the bottom of the shaft were afterwards brought to the surface and placed in a hay-loft which had been arranged as an infirmary. Amid scenes of the most heartrending description the eight men who had been found alive were brought to bank, but from that moment the exploring party could perceive no sign of life below. Some of the explorers heard men calling beyond the falls, but after-damp and the state of the pit prevented further progress and the rescue parties were recalled while clearing was carried on. The distances to which fragments of the dead were blown show that the force of the explosion must have been terrific, but it is uncertain as yet whether it was due to gas mixed with coal-dust or to coal-dust alone. As time went on nine more injured men were discovered.

Trapped underground

In 1862, a pumping engine fell down the single shaft of Hartley Colliery in Northumberland. It blocked the only way out, and 204 men and boys died underground. After this terrible accident a new law was passed, forcing mine owners to make sure that all mines had two shafts, not one.

Workers unite!

In 1851, about 15 million men and women worked for cash wages. Many were poorly paid and treated badly by employers. **Trade unions** helped workers to join together, making them better able to bargain for higher pay and improved working conditions.

Ill-paid and ill

Visiting factory towns, **reformers** were horrified. One found a family of stocking-weavers in Leicestershire earning just 11 shillings (55p) a week between them. Parents and children slept on a shed floor, eating bread and porridge for most meals. In Staffordshire, pottery workers had to dip clay pots into poisonous mixtures of lead and arsenic. It made them too ill to move their fingers.

Factory owners kept wages low in order to sell goods more cheaply than rival firms. Any workers daring to **strike** for higher wages found themselves **sacked** and penniless. Branded as 'troublemakers', they found it hard to get new jobs. On farms, too, wages stayed low. Many farm workers lived in **tied cottages**, and were turned out of their homes if farmers sacked them.

The Tolpuddle Martyrs

The first union was set up in 1834 by Robert Owen (see pages 20 and 21). That year, two members of his Grand National Consolidated Trade Union went to Dorset, where farm workers were protesting about a pay cut from 9 shillings (45p) to 6s (30p) a week. Six of the Dorset men, from the village of Tolpuddle, agreed to start a union, but swore to keep it secret. Trade unions were lawful; secret societies were not. The men were arrested, tried and **transported** to Australia.

Too proud for charity

Joseph Arch formed a union for farm workers in 1872. As a boy he had watched farm labourers line up for 'charity soup' from the parson's wife. Joseph Arch's mother looked 'sad as she watched the little children toddle past, carrying the tin cans, and their toes coming out of their boots'. She told him 'Ah, my boy…you shall never, never do that…'

They became known as the 'Tolpuddle Martyrs' (a martyr is someone who suffers or dies for his or her beliefs). There was such an outcry in Britain that after two years the 'Tolpuddle Martyrs' were brought home.

Robert Owen's union grew to 400,000 members before it failed. More successful was the Amalgamated Society of Engineers (1851), whose members paid 1 shilling (5p) a week to join. In return, the union paid those who lost wages because they were sick or on strike. More unions were started, and in 1868 they joined to form the Trades Union Congress. By 1900, two million workers belonged to unions.

This poster from 1889 calls on dock workers to strike. On their own, strikers had little hope of victory. As union members, they could look for support from other workers.

Take a letter

The Victorians were travelling faster than ever before, by train, steamship and later by car. They wanted messages sent faster, too. This need for speed created the modern 'communications industry'. It also created a new kind of shop: the local post office.

Wired up

The first speedy message invention was the **telegraph** of 1837, which sent electrical signals along wires. Soon many towns had telegraph offices, with operators clicking out words in **Morse code**. A message by wire was much quicker than a letter sent by coach or even by train.

An early Victorian postman delivers letters. People working for the General Post Office were proud of its fast, efficient service. The Victorians sent millions of letters, cards and parcels every year.

Bags of postmen

Until 1840, a letter was paid for by the person who received it. That year, a retired teacher named Rowland Hill came up with a simple idea – the stick-on stamp. The first stamps cost one penny, and soon lots more people were sending letters, as well as Christmas cards, birthday cards and picture postcards. Red pillar boxes in the street and postmen on their rounds became familiar sights.

Errands and deliveries

Victorians paid messengers or 'errand boys' to deliver urgent letters and parcels. Often the boys rode bicycles. Delivery boys brought bread, meat or groceries to a back or side door of a house, known as the tradesmen's entrance.

Victorian postmen called several times a day. A London clerk could post a letter at lunchtime, telling his wife he would be late home. The postman would deliver it in late afternoon. Busy post offices had jobs for counter clerks, letter-sorters, parcel handlers and van-drivers, as well as postmen.

The key to neater writing…

Private letters were written by hand. Many people were proud of their clear handwriting, but copying out business letters took ages. The typewriter, an 1868 American invention, was a big help. Using **carbon paper**, a 'typist' could make several neat copies of a letter at one time. By 1880, typists were at work in many offices.

… and a voice on the line

A Scotsman named Alexander Graham Bell (1847–1922) invented the telephone in 1876. Now people far apart could talk along a wire. The telephone created jobs for **engineers** and also for women, who worked in 'exchanges', plugging wires into boards to connect callers to the right number.

Jobs in an island nation

The sea and ships played a big part in Victorian life. Many factory-made goods were sent by sea to be sold abroad. In return, raw materials (such as timber and cotton) and food (such as grain and meat) were shipped in.

Dockers and shipbuilders

Miles of new **docks** were built at ports such as Liverpool and London, including the docks at Tilbury which opened in 1886. Men who loaded goods on to ships were known as stevedores, but many workers unloading ships were unskilled casual labourers paid by the hour. A five-week **strike** by dockworkers in 1889 brought London's port to a standstill.

By 1900, almost 75 per cent of the world's ships were built in British shipyards, in Belfast and along the Mersey, Clyde and Tyne rivers. These yards employed thousands of men, many of them skilled metalworkers who cut, shaped and fixed metal plates together with **rivets**.

Going to sea

Those who sailed on the big ships learned their skills as teenagers. Many had made their first voyage on a fishing boat or sailing ship, battling with canvas sails in rough seas.

Lifeboats and lighthouses

Without modern radio or radar, many Victorian sailors were lost at sea. Unpaid volunteers from fishing villages and seaside towns manned lifeboats that braved stormy seas to rescue people from shipwrecks. The Royal National Lifeboat Institution was founded in 1824. Around Britain's shores, lighthouse keepers tended the oil-burning lamps that guided ships away from dangerous rocks. Life was lonely in a remote lighthouse. Keepers were cut off from the outside world for two months at a time.

This picture shows fishermen hauling up the catch from their net in baskets.

On a steamship, seamen had to learn new ways of sailing. Instead of scrambling to the breeze-blown mast-tops to fix the sails, men toiled deep inside the ship. In the oil and heat of the ship's engine room, they shovelled coal to feed the boilers. They managed thundering engines that turned paddlewheels or propellers pushing the ship along. It was hot, dirty work.

Jobs were created, too, on the new ocean liners. They were like huge floating hotels that carried passengers between Europe and America.

Fishing jobs

All around the coast of Britain fishing boats set out every day from small harbours, some heading for the icy Arctic Ocean. Fishing was (and still is) hard, cold and dangerous work, and most Victorian fishing families had lost somebody at sea. Women and men too old for the boats worked on the quayside, mending fishing nets. They also cleaned and packed fish into boxes and baskets ready to be taken to market.

Shopkeepers

In many Victorian towns and villages, shops stayed open late. Saturday night was often the busiest time for shopkeepers. Most shops were family businesses, but there were new big stores, too.

Buying and selling food

There were no Victorian supermarkets and no refrigerators or freezers at home. People bought fresh food daily from small local shops or markets. In London, there were 700 'cow-dairies', selling milk from cows kept in small fields and sheds in the city. George Barham, son of a London dairyman, started the Express Country Milk Supply Company in 1864. He used the railway to bring milk direct from countryside farms to people's doors.

In food shops, few items were ready-packed. **Grocers** weighed loose tea from a chest and sold it in paper bags. Flour and sugar were sold in this way too. Butter was patted into small blocks with wooden paddles. Bacon was sliced and cheese cut to the customer's order.

Fixing prices

Shopping began to change in the middle of the 19th century. Drapers' shops selling dress material, towels, sheets and stockings started putting price tickets on goods. Before that, the customer had always asked the price and bargained with the shopkeeper.

The pawnbroker's shop

A pawnbroker's shop displayed the sign of three golden balls. Anybody needing money could 'pawn' a watch (or other item of value) by handing it to the pawnbroker in exchange for cash. They were also given a ticket, known as a pledge. If the person returned to the shop with the pledge and repaid the money, they got the item back. If not, the pawnbroker kept and sold it.

All-in stores

In 1872, William Whiteley opened London's first department store. He called it the 'Universal Provider' because it offered everything from home decorating to funerals. In 1895 it sold a railway and a fleet of steamboats to an Indian ruler! Food stores also set up branches all over the country. Chain stores like Thomas Lipton's and The Home and Colonial Stores were familiar in many towns by the 1880s.

Shop workers often slept above the shop – or even under the counter. Their hours were from 6 a.m. until 10 p.m. In 1847, drapers formed an Early Closing Association, allowing them to take half-days off without losing business to a rival. Marshall and Snelgrove, the London department store, was the first shop to offer staff a lunch and tea break. From 1871, Bank Holidays gave shop workers a welcome extra day off.

Many shops, like this butcher's shop, put on lavish displays, particularly at Christmas. Shop workers were trained to be polite. They had to remember that 'the customer is always right'.

Street traders

✣ ✣

Every Victorian town had at least one market, with stalls selling everything from pets to musical instruments. Victorian streets were ringing with noise and bustle. The air was full of the smells of jellied eels, pea soup, hot pies and fresh buns and the cries of street traders.

Costermongers and pedlars

In a typical street market, costermongers sold fruit and vegetables from a barrow, shouting the prices loudly to outdo any rivals. Shoppers strolled among sellers of **flypapers**, walking sticks and old clothes, muffin men, match-girls and flower-sellers. There were Indians selling coloured scarves, Italian ice-cream sellers, **organ-grinders** with their trained monkeys and **quack doctors** selling 'cure-all' tonics!

Along country lanes, **pedlars** tramped with trays and baskets, or drove small carts from village to village. John Chamberlain lived in Huntingdonshire in the 1860s. Then aged 65, he went around the local public houses carrying two baskets. In one he had a selection of nuts, cakes and sweets; in the other were small packets of seeds. He chanted: 'Any gentleman want any carrot seeds, onion seeds, parsnip seeds, lettuce seeds, parsley seeds, radish seeds or any Windsor fine peas? What I can't get today I'll bring another day.'

A busy scene at London's Billingsgate Fish Market in 1897. Every morning, wagons trundled into the city with fish, meat, fruit, vegetables and flowers for the markets. Cattle, sheep, pigs and geese were driven through town on their way to market.

Street traders selling 'fancy wares'. As Londoners walked through the city streets they could have a shoeshine, buy matches or flowers, and munch a fresh muffin.

Robert Hicks was a Gloucestershire pedlar in the 1890s. He lived in his cart and sold donkeys, salt and sand. Gypsies often called from house to house, selling herbs, flowers, clothes pegs or 'lucky charms' and offering to tell maids' fortunes.

Vanished traders

The warrener protected a wild rabbit warren from foxes, stoats and other predators. He killed and sold the rabbits for meat at the local market. At the same market, a snake catcher with a sack full of live adders might sell snake-fat ointment to ease backaches. Neither is seen any more. Nor is the sandman, who sold fine sand for dusting on a letter to dry the ink. Even the rag and bone man, who collected unwanted household items, is rarely heard calling in the streets today.

Street cries to advertise

Each street-seller had a cry to advertise their goods. Flower-sellers cried 'All a-growing and blooming' or 'Who will buy my sweet lavender?'. 'Cockles and mussels', 'scissors to grind', 'old chairs to mend, rush and cane bottom', 'catch 'em alive' (for sticky flypapers) were all familiar cries heard in bustling Victorian streets.

Servants

More than one million Victorians had jobs in the homes of richer people. Many were women, working as cooks, children's nurses and housemaids. To run the large house of a rich landowner there might be twenty or more servants, both men and women. Less grand families might have just one servant, a 'maid of all work'.

Top and bottom jobs

In a big country house, the butler was head manservant. He took charge of the **pantry** and made sure that food and drink were served properly in the dining room. The head woman servant was the housekeeper. She was in charge of all the maids, who cleaned and dusted the house.

Each servant had his or her own job. Footmen waited at table and opened carriage doors for visitors. Valets helped the master to dress and cared for his clothes. Out of doors, **gamekeepers** protected the deer and game birds, such as pheasants, which were kept for hunting and shooting.

Servants usually 'lived in', with rooms in their own part of a big house. They were not allowed fires in their rooms, but could go downstairs to the 'servants' hall' or the kitchen for meals.

All servants had to be polite and obedient. Anyone who left a job without a 'reference' (a letter of praise from his employer) found it hard to get another one.

The servants' menu

A typical weekly menu for servants' dinners at a country house was: Sunday, roast beef and plum pudding; Monday, cold meat or meat pie, and rice pudding; Tuesday, roast mutton (sheep-meat) and apple pudding; Wednesday, boiled beef, dumplings and cabbage; Thursday, pea soup and **bubble and squeak**; Friday, Irish stew and fruit; Saturday, leg of mutton.

On and off duty

A servant's day started early, fetching water for washing and lighting fires before breakfast. From breakfast to bedtime, a servant would listen for the bell that meant 'come here quickly'. Despite the hard work, many workers 'in service' in a grand house were not badly off. They were well fed and they had entertainment (such as Christmas parties and dances). Life could be more fun than toiling in a factory or being the only, overworked servant in a small house. Charles Dickens described the plight of a maid working on her own in his book *The Old Curiosity Shop*: 'She never went out … or had a clean face, or looked out of any of the windows … or had any rest or enjoyment whatever'.

Rich families kept a horse-drawn carriage. Many people also rode horses. Grooms looked after the horses in the stables, while coachmen drove the carriages. From the 1880s, after cars were invented, some coachmen became car-drivers or chauffeurs.

Empire-builders

There were jobs in the **British Empire** for soldiers, sailors, **civil servants**, **engineers** and merchants. They guarded its frontiers and **trade** routes, ran its government and schools, and built roads, railways, bridges and harbours. Some 'empire-builders' spent years in India or Africa, before returning home to Britain. Others made new lives in Australia, Canada or New Zealand.

Life on the ocean waves

Britain's trade routes were patrolled by warships of the Royal Navy. Boys joined the Navy in their teens, eager for adventure. Sailors were often pictured in advertisements as 'Jolly Jack Tars' in canvas trousers, blue jackets and black hats. In the 1830s, sailors went to sea in wooden sailing ships. By the 1890s, the Navy had ironclad (metal-armoured) steamships, firing much bigger guns.

Soldiers relaxing off duty in India. British soldiers could be found anywhere in the Empire, from Canada to China.

'A soldier's life is terrible hard'

A soldier's life had less appeal than a sailor's, and the British Army was always short of troops. Victorians called the Army the 'thin red line' because most soldiers wore red uniforms. Towards the end of Victoria's reign, battle uniform was changed to khaki (sandy-brown), making troops less easy to pick out as targets.

In peacetime, soldiers spent most of their time in barracks, cleaning their kit and training. Training meant hours of drill (marching for the infantry; parading on horses for the cavalry). Pay was poor, food bad and discipline harsh. Men could be flogged (whipped) for breaking rules. A rich man could buy his way into a regiment as an officer, but many did not take soldiering seriously. Only engineers or artillery officers had proper training.

During the **Crimean War** (1853–56), people were shocked by newspaper stories of awful Army hospitals, where soldiers were cold, hungry and dying of sickness. At the Battle of Balaclava in 1854, confused orders sent 676 Light Brigade horsemen charging straight into Russian cannons. More than 250 men were killed. The disaster caused a national outcry in Britain.

In the 1870s, conditions in the Army were improved. Flogging was ended, and training got better. After six years, a man could leave the Army, but remain 'in reserve', ready to be called up for action if needed.

Boy soldiers

The Victoria Cross, founded in 1856, is Britain's highest award for 'conspicuous bravery' in war. The two youngest soldiers to win it were just fifteen years old. Andrew Fitzgibbon, a hospital **apprentice** in a medical unit, won his Victoria Cross at a fort in China in 1860. Thomas Flinn, a drummer-boy from Athlone in Ireland, won his medal at Cawnpore (Kanpur) in India in 1857.

Writers and artists

With no television, radio, cinema or computers, Victorians had plenty of time for reading. Free lending libraries were set up after 1850, but before then people had to pay to borrow library books. Reading was very popular, especially of poems and long novels such as those by the Brontë sisters, George Eliot, William Thackeray, Thomas Hardy and Charles Dickens. Their novels, which many people still read today, contain descriptions of Victorian people and jobs. Some highlighted the plight of underpaid and ill-treated workers, so helping to bring about changes to the law.

Rags to riches

Some Victorian writers were as famous as any celebrities today. Charles Dickens was one. He worked very hard. His son said that the author wrote 'like a city clerk', scratching away every day with pen on paper in 'businesslike regularity'. Charles Dickens' books, starting with *Pickwick Papers* (1837), made him rich and famous. He toured Britain and America, reading to audiences from his books. Dickens also knew all about poverty. His father was often short of money, and as a boy the author had spent a miserable time at work, pasting labels on bottles in a factory.

This painting by George Cruikshank shows people enjoying the fresh air and entertainment of a Victorian Derby Day. A day at the races brought rich and poor together in their thousands.

Fact and fiction

Nearly all of Charles Dickens' characters have a job, clearly described in his books. In his pages, we meet washerwomen, actors, pickpockets, barbers, detectives, schoolmasters, railwaymen, clerks and lawyers … the list is endless.

In *Oliver Twist*, the young orphan Oliver is taken to work for Mr Sowerberry, an **undertaker**. Escorting Oliver Twist is Mr Bumble, who comments that coffins seem to be getting smaller. Mr Sowerberry laughs: 'There's no denying that … the coffins are somewhat narrower and more shallow than they used to be; but we must have some profit, Mr Bumble.'

Painters and photographers

Few Victorian artists found wealthy people to support them. Most had to sell their paintings to earn a living. Some drew pictures for books. Others painted rich people's portraits, or captured the movement and colours of everyday life at the races, railway station or ironworks. Victorians liked pictures in their homes, especially those of flowers, children, religious scenes and animals.

From the 1840s, after the invention of the camera, there was a new job – the photographer. Photographers did a busy trade and soon every town had at least one studio where families could have their photos taken. Photographers also pictured people at work.

DERBY DAY: ON THE COURSE. PAINTED BY GEORGE CRUIKSHANK.

How do we know?

The Victorian age was the first in history to leave us photographs, moving film and rather crackly sound recordings. Early photographers of the 1840s took posed pictures of people at work or at home. Cameras were later taken everywhere. So we can see Victorians doing many jobs such as ploughing with oxen, driving wagons or sawing timber.

Written evidence

The Victorians also left books, government reports, diaries and letters. Factory records tell us how much people were paid; account books from country houses even show what the servants ate.

People noted the rapid change in how work was done. 'When I first entered this city, the whole of the machinery was executed [done] by hand', said William Fairbairn, who ran an engineering works in Manchester, in 1861. 'Now, everything is done by machine tools with a degree of accuracy which the unaided hand could never accomplish'.

Thousands of people visited London's **Great Exhibition** of 1851. This was Victorian Britain on show, with every marvel of the factory age and goods and inventions from all over the **British Empire**. We know about the exhibition through pictures, newspaper reports and visitors' own memories.

The government began sending out inspectors to check on conditions in factories and mines. Their reports and those of **reformers** tell us how long people worked, how much they were paid, what tools they used and so on. Since 1801 there has been a national **census** every ten years, telling us where people lived, how big families were and what jobs people did.

Things to see

You can still find a lot of evidence for Victorian jobs. You can visit 'working museums', with machinery that recreates coal mines, pottery factories and textile mills. In many towns and villages, there are Victorian factory buildings, and other reminders of the past. All this evidence will help you to build up a picture of just how hard people worked in Victorian times, and how many skills they used in their everyday lives.

This is a 19th-century farm **smock**. Although worn for farm work, smocks were made with great care. Most Victorian workmen wore a cap, jacket, shirt and trousers; women worked in long dresses, often with an apron and a bonnet or scarf on their heads.

Timeline

1824	Workers are legally allowed to form **trade unions**
1830	Liverpool and Manchester Railway opens, the first steam passenger railway
1833	Factory **Act** bans children under nine years of age from working in factories
1834	First trade union is set up by Robert Owen Tolpuddle Martyrs are **transported** to Australia, but later pardoned
1837	Victoria becomes queen
1842	New law stops women and children under the age of ten working underground in coal mines
1847	First 'Ten-Hour Act' reduces working day in parts of the textile industry for women and children under eighteen
1848	First Public Health Act becomes law
1851	The **Great Exhibition** is held in London The first successful trade union, the Amalgamated Society of Engineers, is formed
1853–56	**Crimean War** is fought against Russia
1857	Indian Mutiny, known in India as the Great Rebellion
1865	**Anaesthetic** surgery **pioneered** by Joseph Lister
1867	Factory Act limits the working day in all places of manufacturing that employ more than 50 people
1868	First meeting of the Trades Union Congress in Manchester
1871	Parliament passes a law making trade unions legal
1876	Alexander Graham Bell invents the telephone
1885	Karl Benz of Germany builds his first motor car
1897	Law allows workers to claim **compensation** for injury or sickness caused by work for the first time
1901	Queen Victoria dies. Her son becomes King Edward VII Marconi sends the first radio signals across the Atlantic Ocean.

Sources

Sources (selected)

A Country Camera 1844–1914, Gordon Winter (Penguin, 1973)
Country House Life 1815–1914, Jessica Gerard (Blackwell, 1994)
The Forgotten Arts, John Seymour (DK/National Trust, 1984)
Lark Rise to Candleford, Flora Thompson, (Penguin, 2000)
Oxford Illustrated History of Britain, ed. Kenneth O Morgan
(OUP, 1984)
A Social and Economic History of Industrial Britain, John Robottom
(Longman, 1986)
The Victorian Railway, Jack Simmons (Thames and Hudson, 1991)
Victorian Things, Asa Briggs (Penguin, 1990)
Victorian Village Life, Neil Philip (Albion Press, 1993)
Women in Science, Marilyn Bailey Ogilvie (M.I.T., 1986)

Further reading

Victorian Britain, Andrew Langley (Heinemann, 1994)
Victorian Children, Jane Shuter (Heinemann, 1995)
Victorian Factories, Andrew Langley (Heinemann, 1996)

Also, look on www.heinemannexplore.co.uk for more information
on the Victorians.

Places to visit

Blists Hill Open-Air Museum, Telford, Shropshire
Bradford Industrial and Horses at Work Museum, Yorkshire
Dock Museum, Barrow in Furness, Cumbria
New Lanark Visitor Centre, Lanark, Scotland
North of England Open-Air Museum, Beamish, Co. Durham
Port Sunlight Heritage Centre, Merseyside
Science Museum (London) and Museum of London

Your local tourist information office can tell you about other places
in your area.

Glossary

Act law made to improve working conditions in factories

anaesthetic painkilling drug used in hospitals during operations

apprentice trainee worker, learning a trade

beggars people asking for money from passers-by in the street

British Empire countries ruled by Britain or linked to it (from the late 17th century to the mid-20th century)

bubble and squeak mixed potato and vegetables fried in a pan

carbon paper inked paper used for making copies of a letter

census official population count collecting information about people

cesspit hole beneath a toilet that has no drains attached to it

cholera dangerous disease, caused by drinking water with germs in

civil service/civil servants organization that carries out the day-to-day work of government. Those who work in the civil service are called civil servants.

coke type of fuel for burning, made by heating coal to drive out gases

commuters workers who travel some distance to their place of work

compensation money awarded to someone to make up for a loss or damage to something

Crimean War war fought by Britain, France and Turkey against Russia (1853–56)

docks place where ships are loaded, unloaded and repaired

engineer someone who makes things: a mechanical engineer, for example, makes and works with machinery

flypapers sticky papers sold to catch houseflies

Great Exhibition enormous exhibition of arts and sciences, held at Hyde Park in London in 1851

grocer shopkeeper who sells all kinds of foods

Industrial Revolution great changes in manufacturing and machinery beginning in the 1700s but mainly taking place in Victorian times

locomotive railway engine able to move by itself, and pull a train

loom machine for making cloth

middle class social group made up of people in between the rich (upper class) and the poor (working class)

midwives women who help mothers during childbirth

Morse code code system of dots and dashes invented by the American Samuel Morse and used to send messages by telegraph

organ-grinder man who played a musical machine called a barrel organ by turning a handle, often using a trained monkey to collect money

oxen cattle used to pull ploughs or carts

pantry storeroom for provisions and cutlery in a big house

pedlar trader who travelled about carrying small goods for sale

pioneer someone who is the first to do something

poaching killing wild animals such as deer, pheasants or rabbits on someone else's land

porter worker paid to carry bags for travellers

quack doctor person who makes or sells useless medicines, such as coloured water

quill pen pen made from a goose's or other bird's feather

reformer person who tries to change something to improve it

rivetting joining metal plates together with hammered bolts, called rivets

sacked to be dismissed from one's job

seamstress woman who sews and makes clothes

shift allotted working time in a factory or mine

slums poor areas of bad housing, lacking clean water

smock knee-length shirt-like garment, worn by country working men

stationmaster person in charge of a railway station

strike refusing to work

suburbs residential areas a little way out from the centre of town

tailor man who makes men's clothes

telegraph system for sending messages along wires by electrical impulses

threshing separating grain from wheat stalks, either by machine or by beating the stalks with a weight on a chain, called a flail

tied cottages homes for workers belonging to their employer; the home went with the job

trade buying and selling goods

trade unions organizations of workers, set up to try and get better pay and working conditions

transported punished for a crime by being sent to a different country

typing using a typewriter, a machine with keys pressing on an inked ribbon

undertaker someone who organizes the funeral of a dead person

upper class member of the aristocracy or someone who is rich and powerful – a factory owner, for instance

vaccinate protect someone from getting a disease by giving them an injection or pill

viaduct arched bridge carrying a railway across a valley

workhouse building used to house old, poor and jobless people

working class in Victorian times, people who worked on farms, mines, docks, factories or at home, usually for low wages

Index